UNLOCK YOUR TRUE POTENTIAL

PATH TO PROFESSIONAL GROWTH

NAVNEET SOTA

Copyright © 2023 Navneet Sota

For permissions requests, write to the author at the e-mail navneetsota@gmail.com

Disclaimer: The information in this book is provided for general informational and educational purposes only and is not a substitute for professional advice. While the author and publisher have made every effort to ensure that the information in this book was correct at press time, the author and publisher do not assume and hereby disclaim any liability to any party for any loss, damage, or disruption caused by errors or omissions, whether such errors or omissions result from negligence, accident, or any other cause.

First Edition: October, 2023

Dedication

To my Family: You've been my unwavering support and the foundation of my dreams. Similar to the chapters within these pages, your love and encouragement have shaped my journey of growth and achievement.

To my mentors Rohini, Khushali, Deepa Di and teachers: You've instilled in me the essence of personal development, mirroring the core theme of this book. Each chapter imparts practical wisdom reflecting your guidance, shaping not only this book but, more importantly, my character.

To my mentors for Life, Satish, Krasimir, Vishal, and Tracey: In your mentorship, I recognized the hallmarks of effective leadership—the ability to inspire, collaborate, and persevere. Just as these pages focus on leadership, you've shown me that true leadership surpasses titles, emphasizing the power of vision and unity.

To my Friends, Clients, and Students: My experiences with them have profoundly influenced this book. They propelled me to share these learnings with the world, knowing they've impacted many lives and can further resonate with countless readers both professionally and personally.

Your collective influence is interwoven into this book, symbolizing the transformative journey within these chapters. As we explore self-awareness, resilience, effective communication, and leadership, your wisdom echoes through every word.

With heartfelt gratitude,
Navneet Sota

Contents

BEFORE WE BEGIN

"The journey of a thousand miles begins with one step."

- Lao Tzu

Welcome to "Unlock Your True Potential: The Path to Professional Growth" a book for professionals who aspire to achieve more in their lives and work. Whether you are a beginner or an expert, a student or a leader, a dreamer or a doer, this book is designed to help you discover and unlock your potential for excellence. In today's fast-paced and rapidly evolving world, young professionals face unique challenges and opportunities in their personal and career growth. 'Unlock Your True Potential' offers a comprehensive guide to empower aspiring leaders with the essential skills, knowledge, and mindset needed to excel in their chosen profession and embark on a successful journey of self-improvement.

> *"As you think, so you become. Let your thoughts be noble and your actions righteous, for true personality development lies in the purity of heart and mind."*
>
> *— Shrimad Bhagavad Gita*

Within the pages of this book, we embark on a transformative journey, exploring a wide range of topics centered on personal growth, professional advancement, and effective leadership. Each chapter is meticulously designed to offer practical insights and actionable strategies that will propel you, the young professional, toward excellence.

At the heart of this journey lies personal development — an exploration of self-discovery and self-mastery. It entails understanding your strengths, acknowledging your limitations, and setting a course for continuous improvement. As the foundation of your growth, personal development is the first step towards achieving your goals.

Effective communication is another cornerstone of personal and career success. In a world marked by constant connectivity and communication, the ability to convey ideas, engage with others, and build meaningful relationships is paramount. Effective communication transcends the exchange of words; it's a dynamic force that shapes perceptions and drives success.

Leadership, too, plays a vital role in your journey. It isn't confined to formal titles or positions of authority; it embodies a mindset and a set of skills accessible to all. Effective leadership involves inspiring others, fostering collaboration, and navigating challenges with wisdom. It's about envisioning a brighter future and rallying individuals around a shared vision.

Personal and career growth is a dynamic and ever-evolving process. It's a unique and personal journey marked by challenges and triumphs, setbacks and achievements. It's a journey of self-discovery within a world teeming with opportunities for those willing to seize them.

In the chapters ahead, we will delve into facets such as self-awareness, goal setting, resilience, and embracing change.

We will explore the intricacies of networking, adaptability, and the art of constructive feedback. Strategies for fostering innovation, cultivating a growth mindset, and leading with empathy and integrity will also be covered.

Each chapter introduces practical exercises, offers real-life examples, and presents thought-provoking challenges. It's about applying knowledge in your daily life and work, cultivating habits that drive personal and career success, one step at a time.

This book is your steadfast companion, guiding you through challenges, celebrating your achievements, and reminding you of the immense potential within you. As Albert Einstein wisely said, "The only source of knowledge is experience." Our journey is practical, and firmly grounded in real-world experiences and actionable strategies.

So, as we embark on this transformative voyage, prepare yourself for an inspiring and empowering adventure. Turn the page, dive into the chapters ahead, and let the journey commence — a journey that will shape not only your career but also enrich your life. Together, we will navigate the path to personal and career excellence, illuminating the way for future generations of leaders, dreamers, and doers.

1

The Pillars of Personal Growth

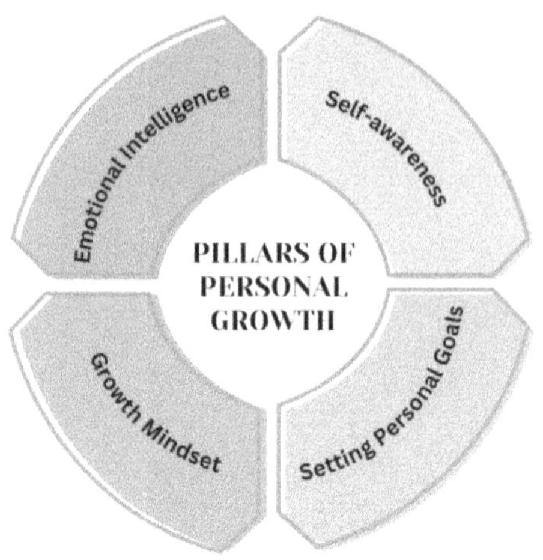

Building a Strong Foundation for Self-Improvement and Fulfillment

"The key to personal development is being proactive. Take responsibility for your own growth, embrace continuous learning, and be the driver of your own success."

- Stephen Covey

In this chapter, we lay the groundwork for personal development, exploring the key pillars that form the foundation of growth for young professionals. From cultivating self-awareness to fostering a growth mindset, participants will learn how to unlock their full potential and embark on a journey of continuous self-improvement.

Topics covered include:

1. Understanding Self-Awareness:

a) The significance of self-awareness in personal and professional development.

b) Techniques for self-reflection and self-assessment to gain insights into strengths and areas for improvement.

<u>Arjuna's Self-Realization in the Bhagavad Gita</u>

In the Bhagavad Gita, a sacred text of Indian mythology, the warrior prince Arjuna experiences a profound moment of self-awareness prior to the Kurukshetra War. He reflects on his duty as a warrior and the moral dilemmas he faces. Krishna, his charioteer and guide, helps him realize his true purpose and align his actions with his duty as a warrior. This example illustrates the transformative potential of self-awareness in making conscious decisions and fulfilling one's responsibilities.

Self-awareness is the ability to recognize and understand your own emotions, thoughts, values, strengths, and weaknesses. It is also the ability to see how your actions affect others and the world around you. It is essential for personal growth, success, happiness, and fulfillment.

Why is self-awareness important? Because it empowers you to:

1. Know Yourself Better:

   a) Identify your passions, talents, goals, and purpose in life.

   b) Acknowledge your limitations, mistakes, and areas of improvement.

   c) Learn from your experiences and feedback from others.

2. **Manage Yourself Better.**

    a) Regulate your emotions, thoughts, and behaviors in different situations.

    b) Cope with stress, challenges, and conflicts.

    c) Make better decisions and choices that align with your values and goals.

3. **Relate to Others Better.**

    a) Empathize with others, understand their perspectives, and communicate effectively.

    b) Foster trust, respect, and rapport with others.

    c) Work well in teams and collaborate with others.

How can you <u>improve</u> your self-awareness? Here are some valuable tips:

1. Ask Yourself Questions.

    a) Regularly reflect on your feelings, thoughts, actions, and their outcomes.

    b) Ask yourself: What am I feeling? Why am I feeling this way? What am I thinking? How are my thoughts influencing my actions? What are the consequences of my actions? How can I grow from this?

2. Seek Feedback.

    a) Request for honest and constructive feedback from others who know you well.

    b) Listen to their opinions and perspectives without being defensive or judgmental.

    c) Learn from their insights and suggestions, resisting the urge to believe you know everything.

3. Take Personality Tests.

    a) Take online or offline tests that measure your personality traits, strengths, weaknesses, preferences, and styles.

b) Consider tools like the Myers-Briggs Type Indicator (MBTI), the StrengthsFinder 2.0, or the DISC assessment. These tests can help you discover more about yourself and how you interact with others.

4. **Read Books.**

   a) Read books that inspire you, challenge you, or teach you something new.

   b) Books expand your knowledge, broaden your perspective, and ignite your imagination. They also help you relate to the stories and experiences of others. Some examples of books that can enhance your self-awareness are: "You Can Win" by Shiv Khera, "The 7 Habits of Highly Effective People" by Stephen Covey, "The Power of Now" by Eckhart Tolle, and "Emotional Intelligence" by Daniel Goleman.

5. **Meditate.**

   a) Meditate regularly to calm your mind, body, and spirit.

   b) Meditation can help you focus on the present moment, observe your thoughts and emotions without judgment. Meditation can also reduce stress, anxiety, and negative emotions.

Remember, self-awareness is not a one-time event but a lifelong journey. It demands constant practice, learning, and improvement. If you want to be a great person, you must be committed to developing your self-awareness and applying it in your life.

"The difference between a great man and a little man is their commitment to integrity and hard work."

— Shiv Khera

---

2. Embracing a Growth Mindset:

a) The power of a growth mindset in driving success and resilience.

b) Strategies to shift from a fixed mindset to a growth-oriented perspective.

Ritesh Agarwal, the founder and CEO of OYO Rooms, an Indian entrepreneur embodies a growth mindset. Starting with a single-budget hotel in 2013, Agarwal expanded OYO into a global hospitality brand. He displayed resilience in overcoming challenges, learning from failures, and adapting to changing market conditions. His continuous quest for innovation and his willingness to evolve have driven OYO's rapid growth, making it one of the world's largest hotel chains, showcasing a remarkable growth mindset.

Growth mindset is the belief that you can improve your abilities, intelligence, and performance through dedicated effort, learning, and feedback. It is the opposite of a fixed mindset, which is the belief that you are born with certain traits or talents that cannot be changed. People with a growth mindset are more likely to embrace challenges, persist in the face of setbacks, seek feedback, and learn from their mistakes. They are also more likely to achieve success, happiness, and fulfillment in life.

Why is a growth mindset important? Because it helps you to:

a) Unlock your potential. Discover and develop your passions, strengths, and talents. Overcome your limitations, weaknesses, and fears. Set and achieve ambitious goals that align with your purpose and values.

b) Adapt to change. Cope with uncertainty, complexity, and diversity in the world. Embrace new opportunities, technologies, and trends. Learn from different people, cultures, and perspectives.

c) Create value. Contribute to your organization, industry, and society. Innovate, solve problems, and create a positive impact. Inspire, influence, and empower others.

How can you develop a growth mindset? Here are some tips:

a) **Change your self-talk.** Pay attention to how you talk to yourself in your mind. Replace any negative thoughts with positive affirmations. For example,

- Instead of saying "I can't do this", say "I can learn how to do this".

- Instead of saying "This is too hard", say "This is a challenge that will make me grow".

- Instead of saying "I'm not good enough", say "I'm worthy of success".

b) **Seek feedback.** Ask for honest and constructive feedback from others who can help you improve. Listen to their opinions and suggestions without being defensive or judgmental. Learn from their insights and experiences.

c) **Take action.** The best way to adopt a growth mindset is to, well, just do it

- At work, take on tasks you have never done before.

- Accept criticism and use it to improve.

- Allocate 20 minutes each day to work on a new skill – and work on it every day, no matter how successful you are at first. The more you take action, the easier it will get.

d) **Celebrate progress.** Recognize and appreciate your efforts and achievements. Take a moment to celebrate every small win and milestone along the way. Reward yourself for your hard work and dedication. Additionally, share your success stories with others who support you.

e) **Learn from failure.** Don't be afraid to fail or make mistakes. Failure is not a sign of weakness or incompetence; it is an opportunity to learn and grow. Take time to analyze what went wrong and what you can do better next time. Remember, don't dwell on the past; focus on the future.

Growth mindset is not a fixed trait that you either have or don't have; it is a choice that you can make every day. If you want to experience more success, happiness, and fulfillment in your life, you must consciously choose a growth mindset.

"Whatever you hold in your mind on a consistent basis is exactly what you will experience in your life."

- Tony Robbins

---

3. Setting Personal Goals:

a)   The importance of setting SMART goals for personal growth.

b)   Methods to create a well-defined action plan to achieve these goals.

Dale Carnegie believed that personal development is the key to success and happiness. He famously stated, "Success is getting what you want. Happiness is wanting what you get"

To achieve what you desire, it's crucial to have a clear vision of your desired outcome and a plan to make it a reality. That's where a career development plan comes in.

If you are a professional who wants to grow into a managerial position or reach the next level in your career, you stand to benefit greatly from creating a career development plan. A career development plan is a personal tool that helps you define your career goals, identify your strengths and weaknesses, and outline the steps you need to take to achieve your objectives.

One of the most effective ways to create a career development plan is to follow the SMART framework, which stands for **Specific, Measurable, Achievable, Relevant, and Timely.** This framework can help you make sure your goals are clear, realistic, and aligned with your values and aspirations.

Here are some tips and examples on how to use the SMART framework in your career development plan:

Specific: Your goals should be clear and well-defined. For instance,

a)   Instead of saying, "I want to be a better leader," you could say, "I want to improve my communication, delegation, and feedback skills."

b)   Instead of saying, "I want to learn a new language," be precise and say, "I want to learn Spanish."

Measurable: Your goals should have criteria to track your progress and evaluate your results. For example,

a) Measure your goal of improving your leadership skills by considering the number of people you manage, the feedback you receive, or the projects you complete.

b) Gauge your goal of learning Spanish by the number of words you learn, the level of proficiency you achieve, or the conversations you engage in.

Achievable: Your goals should be realistic and within your reach. They should challenge you but not overwhelm you. For example,

a) If you are a junior accountant with two years of experience, it may not be achievable to become a CFO in two years. You may need to adjust your timeline or break down your goal into smaller achievable steps.

b) Similarly, if you have no prior knowledge of Spanish, it may not be achievable to become fluent in six months. You may need to adjust your timeline or break down your goal into smaller achievable steps.

Relevant: Your goals should align with your values, interests, and career aspirations. They should also meet the needs and expectations of your employer or industry. For example,

a) If you are passionate about sustainability, your goal of improving your leadership skills should focus on leading green initiatives or projects.

b) If you are interested in traveling to Spain, your goal of learning Spanish should be relevant to your travel plans.

Timely: Your goals should have specific deadlines or timeframes that motivate you to take action. Additionally, they should also be flexible enough to accommodate changes and challenges along the way. For example,

a) You might set a two-year deadline for your goal of improving your leadership or Spanish skills, while also taking time to review and revise your plan every six months.

To create your own career development plan, consider the following steps:

1. **Assess your current situation:** Begin with a self-evaluation to understand where you are now in your career and what areas you need to improve. You can use various tools such as self-assessment tests, feedback surveys, performance reviews, or SWOT analysis (Strengths, Weaknesses, Opportunities, Threats) to identify your skills, interests, values, personality type, achievements, challenges, and opportunities.

2. **Set goals and objectives:** Based on your self-assessment, you can choose one or more career or personal goals that reflect your vision for the future. You can use the SMART framework to make sure your goals are Specific, Measurable, Achievable, Relevant, and Timely. You can also prioritize your goals based on their importance and urgency.

3. **Identify actions to achieve your goals:** Once you have your SMART goals, you can break them down further into tasks and to-do lists with deadlines. You can also identify the resources and support you need to complete each task. For example, if one of your tasks is to improve your communication skills, consider enrolling in an online course, reading a book, or joining a Toastmasters club.

4. **Implement your plan:** After planning your actions, it's time to execute them. Employ tools such as calendars, reminders, trackers, or apps to help you stay organized and focused on your tasks. You can also reward yourself for completing each task or milestone to keep yourself motivated.

5. **Review and reassess your plan:** As you work on your plan, it's important to monitor your progress and evaluate your results. You can use various tools such as feedback surveys, performance reviews, or self-reflection exercises to measure how well you are doing and what changes or improvements you need to make. Celebrate your achievements and share them with others.

Here is an example of a professional goal plan for someone who wants to lead a Spanish team in six months, but doesn't speak or understand **the** Spanish language fully:

Goal: To learn Spanish in six months

Why: To effectively communicate and lead a local Spanish team in Spain

How: By studying Spanish vocabulary, grammar, pronunciation, and culture

Tasks:

a) Download **the** Duolingo app and complete one lesson per day

b) Buy 'Easy Spanish Step-by-Step' book and read one chapter per week

c) Watch one episode of La Casa de Papel on Netflix weekly with subtitles

d) Join a Spanish language exchange group on Meetup and attend one meeting per month

e) Listen to one podcast episode of Coffee Break Spanish per week

f) Plan a trip to Spain for the following summer

Resources:

a) App: Duolingo

b) Book: Easy Spanish Step-by-Step

c) Show: La Casa de Papel

d) Group: Meetup

e) Podcast: Coffee Break Spanish

f) Trip: Expedia

Timeline:

a) First Month: Learn 500 words and basic grammar rules

b) Second Month: Learn 1000 words and intermediate grammar rules

c) Third Month: Learn 1500 words and advanced grammar rules

d) Fourth Month: Watch La Casa de Papel without subtitles and understand 80% of the dialogue

e) Fifth Month: Have a 15-minute conversation in Spanish with a native speaker

f) Sixth Month: Take a Spanish proficiency test and score at least B1 level

Evaluation:

a) First Month: Take a vocabulary test and get a score of 80% or higher

b) Second Month: Take a grammar test and get a score of 80% or higher

c) Third Month: Take an advanced grammar test and get a score of 80% or higher

d) Fourth Month: Watch La Casa de Papel without subtitles and write a summary of the episode in Spanish

e) Fifth Month: Record a conversation in Spanish with a native speaker and get feedback on your pronunciation, fluency, and accuracy

f) Sixth Month: Take the DELE exam and get a certificate of B1 level or higher

Remember, your plan is not set in stone. You can always adjust it as you go along, depending on your situation and opportunities. The key is to have a clear vision of your goal and take consistent action to achieve it.

Lord Krishna exhibits exceptional emotional intelligence and empathy while guiding Arjuna through his moral dilemma. Krishna's ability to understand Arjuna's emotions and provide guidance with compassion exemplifies the significance of emotional intelligence in leadership and decision-making.

- Bhagavad Gita

---

4. Developing Emotional Intelligence:

a) The role of emotional intelligence in enhancing interpersonal relationships and decision-making.

b) Practices to cultivate emotional intelligence and empathy.

Emotional Intelligence (EI) is the ability to comprehend and manage not only your own emotions but also those of the people around you. It is a vital skill for anyone who wants to succeed in today's complex and competitive world.

According to **Daniel Goleman**, a psychologist and journalist who popularized the concept of EI, there are four domains of EI: self-awareness, self-management, social awareness, and relationship management. Within each domain, there are 12 competencies that can be learned and developed through practice.

a) **Self-awareness:** This is the ability to recognize and understand your own emotions, strengths, weaknesses, values, and motives. Individuals with high self-awareness are honest with themselves and others. **They** have a clear sense of their goals and purpose.

b) **Self-management**: This involves the ability to control or redirect your emotions, impulses, and moods, and to adapt to changing circumstances. People with strong self-management are optimistic, resilient, and able to handle stress and challenges effectively.

c) **Social awareness**: This is the ability to empathize with others, understand their feelings and perspectives, and appreciate their differences and diversity. Individuals with high social awareness are attentive, respectful, and compassionate, and can read the emotional cues of others.

d) **Relationship management**: This encompasses the ability to build and maintain positive relationships with others, communicate clearly and persuasively, work well in teams, and manage conflict constructively. People with high relationship management are influential, inspiring, and supportive, and can foster trust and cooperation.

Why is EI important for your career and life? Research has shown that EI is a key factor in determining your performance, productivity, satisfaction, and well-being at work. EI can help you:

1. **Enhance your leadership skills**: EI can help you motivate yourself and others, set and achieve goals, make sound decisions, solve problems creatively, and handle difficult situations with grace.

2. **Improve your communication skills**: EI can help you listen actively, express yourself clearly, give and receive feedback effectively, persuade and negotiate successfully.

3. **Strengthen your teamwork skills**: EI can help you collaborate with others, respect diversity, build rapport, manage conflict, and foster trust.

4. **Boost your emotional health**: EI can help you cope with stress, regulate your emotions, develop a positive outlook, and increase your self-esteem.

How can you cultivate EI and empathy? There are numerous methods to improve your EI skills through practice. Consider the following examples:

a) To **increase your self-awareness**: Keep a journal of your thoughts and feelings; ask for feedback from others; take personality or EI tests; reflect on your values and goals; meditate or practice mindfulness.

b) To **improve your self-management**: Set realistic and challenging goals; monitor your progress; reward yourself for achievements; practice positive affirmations; learn relaxation techniques; seek help when needed.

c) To **enhance your social awareness**: Observe the emotions of others; listen with empathy; ask open-ended questions; show interest and curiosity; respect different opinions and perspectives; volunteer for a social cause.

d) To **develop your relationship management**: Express appreciation and gratitude; give constructive feedback; apologize sincerely; assert yourself respectfully; compromise when necessary; celebrate successes.

Imagine being in a warm, cozy apartment with your partner and a pet dog. You work as a teacher in a school that educates children from diverse backgrounds and cultures. You have a lot of passion and dedication for your work, but you also face a lot of challenges and demands from your students, parents, and colleagues.

Then, one day, you receive a phone call from your partner, who tells you that they have been offered a promotion at their job, but it requires them to relocate to another city. You feel happy and proud for your partner, but also sad and anxious about the possibility of leaving your job, your home, and your friends. You are not sure what to do, and you need some time to think.

Your partner senses your mixed emotions and asks you how you feel about their news. You decide to use your emotional intelligence skills to handle this situation. You do the following:

- Acknowledge and name your emotions,

- Cope with your negative emotions in healthy ways,

- Understand and empathize with your partner's emotions,

- Communicate and cooperate with your partner effectively.

For example, you can talk to your partner and share your feelings and concerns; you can listen to their feelings and concerns; you can discuss the pros and cons of their decision; you can explore the options and alternatives; you can support their choice and respect their autonomy; you can make a plan and prepare for the change; you can seek help or advice from others if needed.

By doing these things, you can show your partner that you love them and care about them, and that you value their happiness and success. By doing these things, you handle the situation maturely and respectfully, and strengthen your personal and professional life.

2

Effective Communication in the Digital Age

Mastering Virtual Connections and Influential Communication Strategies

"Effective communication is not about impressing others with your words but connecting with them at a deeper level. Listen empathetically and speak from the heart."

- Dale Carnegie

In this chapter, we delve into the art of effective communication for young professionals in the digital era. From mastering virtual communication to honing presentation skills, participants will learn how to convey ideas with impact and build strong connections with colleagues and clients.

Topics covered include:

1. Navigating Virtual Communication:

a) Overcoming challenges and maximizing opportunities in remote work communication.

b) Best practices for clear and engaging virtual interactions.

2. Power of Active Listening:

a) Understanding the art of active listening and its importance in effective communication.

b) Techniques for practicing attentive listening and empathetic responses.

3. Crafting Compelling Presentations:

a) Elements of a persuasive presentation that captivates audiences.

b) Tips for using visuals and storytelling to make presentations memorable.

4. Effective Feedback and Conflict Resolution:

a) Providing constructive feedback to facilitate growth and improvement.

b) Implementing strategies for resolving conflicts amicably and fostering positive work relationships.

While I had the chance to speak to a very dear friend and a Managing

Director (MD) of a mid-sized company, having operations spanning continents, for this book, given below is an excerpt of the discussion around the topic of **Effective Communication** in today's world.

Me: Greetings! Today, we're in for a treat as we delve into the intriguing journey of our MD friend. Could you share a bit about your early days and the challenges you faced in reaching your current position?

MD: Absolutely! Picture this: small town, limited opportunities, a tight budget. I had to juggle part-time work with studies. The struggles were real - financial constraints, access to quality education, and moments of doubt.

Me: How did effective communication influence your growth personally and professionally?

MD: Communication was key. Early in my career, I realized mastering this skill was vital for networking, persuasion, and idea presentation. It connected me with people from diverse backgrounds and helped convey thoughts clearly.

Me: Fascinating! Can you share an instance where your communication skills made a significant impact on your career?

MD: Ah, the investor presentation! It was more than data; it was about storytelling and connecting with their dreams. Persuasive communication secured the funding we needed.

Me: Amazing! And as you climbed the corporate ladder, how did communication shape your leadership journey?

MD: It became about inspiration and guidance. Clear communication of our vision, values, and goals aligned everyone.

Listening became crucial, fostering trust and collaboration.

Me: Jumping to the digital age, how has it shifted communication within your team and with the world?

MD: Oh, it's a game-changer! Internally, tools like video conferencing enhanced efficiency. Externally, social media broadened our reach and enabled real-time feedback, pushing our strategies to evolve.

Me: Finding the balance between digital tools and face-to-face interactions - how do you do it?

MD: Key is not losing the human touch. Regular in-person or video meetings are a must. And let's not forget training in digital etiquette to preserve genuine connections.

Me: In this fast-paced digital world, any advice on mastering digital communication?

MD: Embrace digital tools, but remember, behind screens are real people. Authenticity and empathy matter. Treat online interactions as you would face-to-face - with respect and care.

Me: Thank you for these golden nuggets of wisdom! Your journey and insights will surely inspire many readers.

Navigating Virtual Communication: Overcoming Challenges and Maximizing Opportunities

In today's digital age, virtual communication has become a cornerstone of modern work life. For IT professionals, remote work and the reliance on digital tools have opened up new possibilities and challenges alike. In this section, we'll delve into the multifaceted realm of virtual communication, exploring both the hurdles it presents and the opportunities it affords.

1. Overcoming Challenges - The transition to remote work has ushered in a set of unique challenges, including:

a) Misinterpretation and Disconnection: Virtual communication often lacks the non-verbal cues we rely on during face-to-face interactions. This can lead to misunderstandings and a sense of disconnection among team members.

b) Time Zone Differences: Collaborating with colleagues or clients across different time zones can create logistical challenges. Balancing work schedules to accommodate everyone requires thoughtful planning.

c) Technical Issues: From internet connectivity problems to glitches in communication platforms, technical issues can disrupt virtual meetings and collaborations.

2. Best Practices for Clear and Engaging Virtual Interactions - Effective virtual communication is an art that, when mastered, can enhance productivity and collaboration. Some best practices include:

a) Clear and Concise Communication: In the virtual realm, clarity is paramount. Ensure your messages and instructions are straightforward and easy to understand. For example, label your email with a clear "Call to Action" subject; [URGENT Response required] / [Need Review] / [Complete by XX-XX], etc

b) Active Engagement: Encourage active participation in virtual meetings. Use interactive tools, polls, and open discussions to keep participants engaged and invested.

c) Visual Aids: Incorporating visual elements, such as slides or infographics, can make presentations more engaging and help convey complex information effectively.

d) **Scheduled Breaks:** Long virtual meetings can be mentally draining. Scheduling short breaks can help maintain focus and energy levels.

e) **Consistent Communication:** Regular updates and check-ins are essential to keep remote teams informed and aligned with project goals.

f) **Cultural Sensitivity:** In a globalized work environment, being mindful of cultural differences and adapting your communication style accordingly fosters a more inclusive and harmonious virtual workspace.

Navigating virtual communication is an ongoing process of adaptation and refinement. By embracing these best practices, professionals can overcome the challenges and capitalize on the vast opportunities that remote work communication offers, ultimately fostering stronger connections and achieving success in the digital age.

Power of Active Listening: Enhancing Communication through Empathetic Engagement

Active listening is an essential component of effective communication, transcending mere hearing to truly understand and engage with others. In this section, we will delve into the art of active listening and its profound significance in fostering meaningful interactions.

The Art of Active Listening and Its Importance

Active listening is more than a passive reception of words; it's a dynamic process that involves focused attention, genuine interest, and empathetic engagement. When we actively listen, we send a powerful message to the speaker: that their words matter, and we value their perspective.

Effective communication relies on active listening for several reasons:

1. **Understanding:** Active listening enables us to grasp the speaker's thoughts, feelings, and intentions accurately. This understanding is the foundation for meaningful responses.

2. **Empathy:** By immersing ourselves in the speaker's perspective, we can empathize with their emotions and experiences. This empathetic connection fosters trust and rapport.

3. **Conflict Resolution:** Active listening is instrumental in resolving conflicts. It allows us to uncover underlying issues, validate concerns, and work collaboratively toward solutions.

Techniques for Attentive Listening and Empathetic Responses

Mastering active listening requires practice and dedication. Here are some techniques to enhance your listening skills:

1. **Maintain Eye Contact:** Establishing eye contact demonstrates your presence and attentiveness. It shows that you are fully engaged in the conversation. Turn on the video in your official calls, and ensure you make your presence felt.

2. **Paraphrase and Reflect:** Periodically summarize the speaker's main points to confirm your understanding. Reflecting their emotions and concerns validates their perspective.

3. **Ask Open-Ended Questions:** Encourage the speaker to elaborate by asking open-ended questions. These questions invite deeper insights and demonstrate your interest.

4. **Avoid Interrupting:** Resist the urge to interrupt or interject your own opinions. Let the speaker express themselves fully before responding.

5. **Non-Verbal Cues:** Use non-verbal cues, such as nodding or leaning in, to convey your engagement. These cues reassure the speaker that

they have your full attention.

Incorporating these techniques into your communication repertoire will not only enhance your active listening skills but also elevate your overall ability to connect, collaborate, and communicate effectively with others. Active listening empowers you to build more profound relationships, resolve conflicts amicably, and inspire trust, ultimately contributing to your personal and professional success.

1. **Crafting Compelling Presentations: The Art of Captivating Your Audience**

Effective presentation skills are indispensable for professionals, as they empower you to convey complex ideas, engage your audience, and drive your message home. In this section, we will explore the key elements of a persuasive presentation that not only capture attention but also leave a lasting impression.

Elements of a Persuasive Presentation

1. **Clarity and Structure:** Start with a clear, well-organized structure. Your presentation should have a compelling introduction, a coherent body with key points, and a memorable conclusion that reinforces your message.

2. **Engaging Content:** Craft your content with your audience in mind. Use language that is accessible and relatable, avoiding jargon whenever possible. Make your message relevant to your listeners.

3. **Storytelling:** Weave a narrative throughout your presentation. Stories resonate with audiences, making information more relatable and memorable.

Tips for Using Visuals and Storytelling

1. **Visual Aids:** Incorporate visuals strategically. Use images, charts, and graphs to illustrate key points and data. Visual aids break the monotony of text-heavy slides and enhance audience comprehension.

2. **Slide Design:** Keep your slides clean and uncluttered. Use a consistent and visually appealing design theme. Limit the use of bullet points and text; instead, use visuals to complement your spoken words.

3. **Story Arc:** Develop a compelling story arc for your presentation. Begin with a relatable scenario or anecdote that draws your audience in. Progress through the narrative, building tension or intrigue, and resolve it with your main message or call to action.

4. **Engagement Techniques:** Interact with your audience. Ask questions, encourage participation, and invite feedback. Engaged listeners are more likely to retain information.

5. **Practice and Rehearse:** Practice your presentation multiple times. Rehearsing not only helps you become more comfortable with the material but also ensures smooth delivery and better timing.

6. **Body Language:** Pay attention to your body language. Maintain eye contact, use gestures purposefully, and vary your tone of voice to convey enthusiasm and confidence.

Crafting compelling presentations is a valuable skill that can set you apart in your career. By incorporating these elements and techniques, you can create presentations that not only inform but also inspire, leaving your audience with a clear understanding of your message and a lasting impression of your expertise.

2. Effective Feedback and Conflict Resolution: Building Stronger Work Relationships

In the fast-paced world, the ability to provide constructive feedback and resolve conflicts amicably is essential for fostering positive work relationships and ensuring a collaborative, productive environment. This section explores the twin pillars of effective feedback and conflict resolution and their pivotal role in professional growth.

Providing Constructive Feedback for Growth - Constructive feedback is a powerful tool for personal and professional development. It creates an environment where individuals can learn from their mistakes, refine their skills, and grow. Key aspects of providing constructive feedback include:

1. **Specificity:** Feedback should be specific and focused on observable behaviors or outcomes. Vague or generalized feedback lacks actionable insights.

2. **Timeliness:** Deliver feedback promptly, ideally close to the observed behavior or action. Timely feedback allows individuals to reflect on their actions and make improvements.

3. **Balance:** Strike a balance between highlighting areas for improvement and acknowledging strengths. Encouragement and affirmation are as important as constructive criticism.

4. **Empathy:** Approach feedback with empathy and understanding. Recognize that individuals may have different perspectives and experiences that influence their actions.

Strategies for Resolving Conflicts Amicably - Conflict is a natural part of any workplace. It can arise from differences in opinions, competing priorities, or misunderstandings. How conflicts are managed can significantly impact work relationships. Strategies for amicable conflict resolution include:

1. Active Listening: Listen attentively to all parties involved in the conflict. Understand their viewpoints and concerns before formulating a response.

2. Open Communication: Encourage open and honest communication. Create a safe space where individuals feel comfortable expressing their concerns.

3. Mediation: In cases of more significant conflicts, consider involving a neutral mediator to facilitate the resolution process.

4. Collaborative Problem-Solving: Collaborate with the parties involved to find mutually acceptable solutions. Focus on common goals and shared interests.

5. Forgiveness and Moving Forward: Once a resolution is reached, emphasize forgiveness and the importance of moving forward positively. Lingering resentment can hinder future collaboration.

Effective feedback and conflict resolution are skills that can be honed over time. They not only lead to personal and professional growth but also foster a harmonious work environment where individuals feel valued, understood, and motivated to contribute their best. In the ever-evolving professional environment, these skills are instrumental in building strong and productive teams.

3

Time Management and Productivity Strategies

Mastering the Clock: Techniques for Efficiency and Goal Achievement

---

Successful people are those who manage their time wisely.

Treat time as your most valuable resource, and you'll see extraordinary results."

- Brian Tracy

I n this Chapter, we explore time management techniques tailored to the demands of young professionals. Participants will discover how to optimize productivity, prioritize tasks, and strike a balance between work and personal life.

Topics covered include:

1. The Importance of Time Management:

a) Understanding the profound impact of effective time management on productivity and well-being.

b) Identifying and overcoming common time-wasting habits that hinder progress.

2. Goal setting for Success:

a) Setting realistic and achievable goals for personal and professional growth.

b) Developing a structured system to track progress and stay on course.

3. Techniques for Productivity and Focus:

a) Implementing strategies to enhance focus, concentration, and overall efficiency at work.

b) Practical tips for minimizing distractions and maintaining peak performance.

4. Achieving Work-Life Balance:

a) Promoting work-life harmony and managing stress in today's competitive world.

b) Techniques for unplugging and recharging to avoid burnout.

1. The Importance of Time Management

In the grand tapestry of personal and professional growth, the art of time management stands as a gentle yet powerful brushstroke, defining the contours of productivity and serenity. Understanding the profound impact of effective time management on both productivity and the quality of life is the cornerstone of any individual's pursuit of success.

Impact on Productivity: Consider the story of Nithin Kamath, the visionary founder of Zerodha, revolutionizing the landscape of stock trading in India. Through judicious time management, he not only built a leading fintech company but also empowered countless individuals to navigate the stock market efficiently. Time, when invested sagely, can yield exponential returns.

Effective time management is akin to composing a melody; it harmonizes the discordant notes of our tasks into a symphony of productivity. By organizing our time around priorities and deadlines, we conduct our lives with precision, reducing the cacophony of stress and anxiety.

Enhancing Well-being: Time management is the gentle maestro orchestrating the concerto of our lives. It provides the baton of control, allowing us to set the tempo of our days. By apportioning time for work, rest, relationships, and personal growth, we cultivate a life that resonates with harmony. This dedicated 'me-time' becomes the cornerstone of our emotional and mental well-being.

Avoiding Time-wasting Habits: To harness the true potential of time management, we must discern and discard the sly saboteurs of time. Procrastination, excessive social media consumption, and failure to delegate can stealthily dissipate our valuable hours. Reflect on your own routines. Are there activities that masquerade as productive but, in truth, drain your time and energy?

Exercise for Effective Time Management:

1. **Inventory of Time:** For a week, keep a time log, jotting down every activity and its duration. At the end of the week, categorize them into productive, non-productive, and essential activities.

 2. **Prioritize and Optimize:** Identify the activities that contribute most to your goals and well-being. Devote more time to these and minimize the non-productive ones. Delegate where possible.

 3. **Create a Time Budget:** Allocate specific time blocks for different activities each day. Stick to this budget diligently and adjust as needed.

2. The Roadmap to Triumph: Goal setting for a Fulfilling Life

Goal setting is similar to plotting a course on a map - it provides direction and purpose, guiding us towards our desired destinations of personal and professional growth. Understanding the art of setting realistic and achievable goals is a fundamental skill in the quest for success.

Setting Realistic and Achievable Goals: Imagine a farmer sowing seeds. Each seed represents a goal. A wise farmer meticulously chooses the seeds based on the soil, weather, and resources available. Similarly, in our journey, we must align our goals with our capabilities, resources, and circumstances. For example, if you aspire to learn a new language, consider your daily time availability and learning capacity realistically. Setting achievable milestones ensures consistent progress, boosting motivation and confidence.

Moreover, break down your goals into smaller, achievable tasks. If your goal is to write a book, start with writing a certain number of words or pages each day. These achievable tasks create a sense of accomplishment, propelling you towards the larger goal.

Developing a Progress Tracking System: Imagine building a puzzle. Each piece represents a step towards your goal. Keeping track of these pieces helps you visualize the progress of completing the puzzle - your goal. Similarly, having a system to track your progress is crucial. It could be a simple journal, an app, or a whiteboard. Regularly update your progress, celebrating milestones achieved and reevaluating the strategy if needed. For instance, if your goal is to improve physical fitness, create a tracking chart to log your daily exercises, weight, or miles jogged. As you see the entries fill up, you'll gain a tangible sense of progress, motivating you to keep going.

Exercise for Effective Goal setting:

1. Vision Board Creation: Collect images, quotes, and symbols representing your goals. Create a vision board by pasting them on a board or a digital platform. This serves as a daily reminder and a source of motivation.

2. SMART Goals Framework: Familiarize yourself with the SMART goals concept - Specific, Measurable, Achievable, Relevant, and Timely. Apply this framework to refine your goals.

3. Weekly Reflection: Set aside time each week to reflect on your progress. Celebrate achievements and adjust your strategies for the upcoming week.

In conclusion, goal setting is the compass guiding us in the vast sea of opportunities. Let us set our sails with realistic objectives, and a well-charted map to navigate our course. With determination and perseverance, we shall reach the shores of triumph, fulfilling both our personal and professional aspirations.

3. Unleashing Your Potential: Mastering Productivity and Focus

In the dynamic realm of modern work, productivity and focus are the twin engines propelling us towards success. Understanding the strategies to enhance focus, concentration, and efficiency is paramount for navigating this fast-paced landscape.

Strategies for Enhancing Focus and Efficiency: Imagine a master painter meticulously bringing a canvas to life, stroke by stroke. Similarly, achieving peak productivity involves deliberate and purposeful actions. Techniques like time blocking, where you allocate specific time blocks for particular tasks, and the Pomodoro Technique, which involves focused work sessions followed by short breaks, are effective methods to enhance focus and productivity.

For example, Sundar Pichai, the CEO of Alphabet Inc., often emphasizes the importance of effective time management and blocking off specific time for priority tasks. This strategy has been instrumental in his career achievements.

Tips for Minimizing Distractions:

Distractions are the adversaries of focus. Establishing boundaries and minimizing interruptions is key. Turn off non-essential notifications, create a dedicated workspace, and communicate your focus times to colleagues. Learning to say no when necessary is also crucial to guard your time and maintain concentration.

Consider the story of Aruna, a successful entrepreneur. She often found herself overwhelmed by constant notifications on her phone. Implementing a strict 'notification-free' period during her work hours significantly improved her productivity and allowed her to focus on her critical tasks.

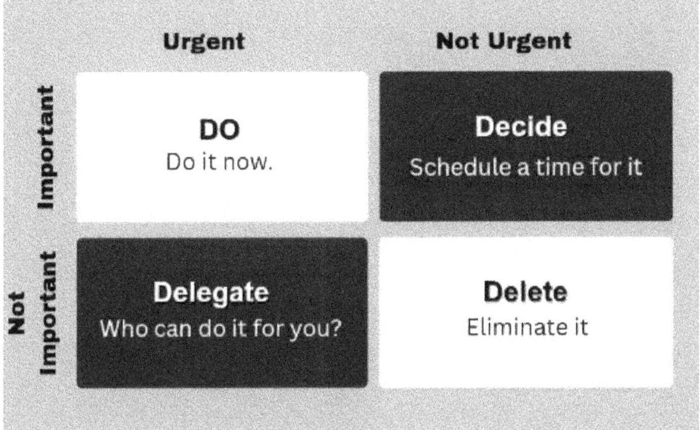

Fig. 3.1

Exercise to Boost Productivity:

1. Mindful Breathing: Begin and end your workday with a brief session of mindful breathing. Sit in a comfortable position, close your eyes, and focus on your breath. This simple exercise calms the mind, enhances focus, and prepares you for a productive workday.

2. Distraction Log: Maintain a log for a day, jotting down every instance you get distracted or interrupted. Note the cause of distraction and its impact on your work. Analyze this log to identify patterns and develop strategies to minimize these distractions.

3. Prioritization Matrix: Create a matrix with two axes: 'Urgent' and 'Important.' List your tasks accordingly and focus on completing those that fall into the ' Urgent, Important' quadrant first. This helps maintain focus on critical tasks.

In conclusion, productivity and focus are the twin stars guiding us through the galaxy of achievements. By adopting these strategies and exercises, we fine-tune our abilities, navigating our journey towards optimal productivity and peak performance in the workplace.

4. Achieving Work-Life Balance: Harmonizing Worlds

In today's bustling professional realm, achieving a harmonious work-life balance is an art worth mastering. Balancing work demands with personal well-being is crucial for long-term success and satisfaction. Understanding the methods to promote this equilibrium and manage stress is pivotal in navigating this fast-paced, demanding environment.

Promoting Work-Life Harmony and Managing Stress:

Picture a tightrope walker gracefully traversing a thin wire. Similarly, achieving work-life harmony requires a delicate balance. Techniques like setting clear boundaries between work and personal time, scheduling regular breaks, and embracing mindfulness can significantly impact stress levels.

For instance, Bill Gates, the co-founder of Microsoft, is known for his emphasis on regular 'think weeks.' He retreats to a quiet place for a week, free from distractions, to reflect and think deeply about the future of technology and Microsoft. This practice not only rejuvenates him but also fuels innovation.

Techniques for Unplugging and Recharging:

Unplugging from work is a crucial skill in the digital age. Techniques like time management, where you allocate specific hours for work and stick to them rigorously, can help in unplugging effectively. Additionally, engaging in hobbies, spending time with loved ones, and pursuing physical activities provide a much-needed recharge.

Consider the story of Ruchi, a software engineer. She dedicated her weekends to her passion for painting. Engaging in this creative outlet provided her with a mental escape from work-related stress and ultimately improved her focus and productivity during the workweek.

Exercise for Balancing Work and Life:

1. Digital Detox Day: Dedicate a day each week to a 'digital detox'. Disconnect from emails, social media, and work-related activities for the day. Instead, focus on activities that bring you joy and relaxation. Observe how this break rejuvenates you and impacts your overall well-being.

2. Prioritize Personal Time: Set aside at least 30 minutes to an hour each day for activities that are solely for personal pleasure. It could be reading, exercising, or spending time with family. Guard this time fiercely, and let it be non-negotiable.

3. Reflect and Adjust: At the end of each week, reflect on how well you managed your work-life balance. Did you honor the boundaries you set? Adjust your strategies for the upcoming week accordingly.

In conclusion, work-life balance is the compass that guides us through our work life. Let us, as professionals, embrace these techniques and exercises, ensuring that our journey is not only successful but also fulfilling on a personal level. By achieving this harmony, we craft a legacy of achievement, well-being, and contentment.

4

Cultivating Leadership Skills

Guiding Principles and Practical Strategies for Effective Leadership

"Leadership is not about being in charge. It's about taking care of those in your charge."

- John C. Maxwell

This chapter delves into the realm of leadership, empowering young professionals with the knowledge and skills to become influential and effective leaders within their organizations.

Topics covered include:

1. Understanding Leadership Styles:

a) Exploring different leadership styles and their unique attributes.

b) Identifying the most suitable leadership approach based on individual strengths and organizational needs.

2. Leading with Vision:

a) The significance of visionary leadership in inspiring and guiding teams.

b) Crafting a compelling vision and communicating it effectively to stakeholders.

3. Building High-Performing Teams:

a) Strategies for fostering teamwork, collaboration, and a positive team culture.

b) Techniques for empowering team members to reach their full potential.

4. Ethical Leadership and Decision-Making:

a) The role of ethical leadership in building trust and credibility.

b) Approaches to ethical decision-making and navigating complex ethical dilemmas.

1. Understanding Leadership Styles: Crafting Leadership Brilliance - Leadership is an art, a symphony where various styles harmonize to

create a melody of effective guidance. Understanding the diverse leadership styles and their unique attributes is essential for every aspiring leader. It's akin to an artist understanding the brushstrokes that shape a masterpiece.

Exploring Different Leadership Styles and Their Attributes: Leadership styles can be compared to colors on a palette, each adding its unique hue to the canvas.

a) Autocratic leadership involves a strong, centralized control.

b) Democratic leadership promotes collaboration and participation.

c) Laissez-Faire leadership grants autonomy to team members.

d) Transformational leadership inspires and motivates.

e) Transactional leadership focuses on structure and rewards.

For instance, consider the leadership style of Mr. Ratan Tata, former Chairman of Tata Sons. His leadership was a blend of transformational and democratic styles. He inspired change and innovation within the Tata Group while fostering a culture of collaboration and participation.

Identifying the Most Suitable Leadership Approach: Just as a wise chef chooses the right ingredients for a dish, a skilled leader selects the appropriate leadership style based on individual strengths and organizational needs. A leader's self-awareness of their strengths, weaknesses, and the organization's culture is fundamental.

An exercise to identify the suitable leadership approach involves self-reflection and feedback. Engage with colleagues, superiors, and subordinates to gather insights into your leadership style. Compare this with the needs and goals of your organization. Understand where your natural inclinations align with the organizational requirements and adapt accordingly.

Exercise for Leadership Self-Awareness:

1. **Leadership Strengths Assessment**: Use leadership assessment tools such as StrengthsFinder, DISC, or the Myers-Briggs Type Indicator (MBTI) to identify your leadership strengths and styles.

2. **360-Degree Feedback**: Seek feedback from peers, subordinates, supervisors, and even external stakeholders. Use their perspectives to understand how your leadership style is perceived and its impact on your team and organization.

3. **SWOT Analysis**: Conduct a SWOT (Strengths, Weaknesses, Opportunities, Threats) analysis of your leadership style. Assess how your style aligns with your organizational goals and where adjustments or enhancements can be made.

In conclusion, understanding the mosaic of leadership styles is the compass guiding us through the dynamic world of leadership. Let us embrace these styles, recognizing their distinctiveness and nuances. By aligning our approach with our innate strengths and the needs of our organization, we create a symphony of leadership brilliance that inspires and drives teams towards a common vision.

2. Leading with Vision: Illuminating the Path

Visionary leadership is akin to being a lighthouse in stormy seas of uncertainty. It's the beacon that guides and inspires teams, creating a sense of purpose and direction. Understanding the significance of visionary leadership and mastering the art of crafting and communicating a compelling vision is the hallmark of a true leader.

The Significance of Visionary Leadership: Imagine a captain charting a course for a voyage. The captain's vision encompasses the destination, the route, and the potential obstacles along the way. Similarly, visionary leadership encapsulates a clear image of the future, a roadmap, and the potential challenges that may arise. This vision fuels motivation, fosters alignment, and steers teams towards shared objectives.

For example, Jeff Bezos, the founder of Amazon, possessed a vision to create the world's most customer-centric company. This vision fueled Amazon's relentless focus on customer satisfaction and propelled the company to the heights it has achieved today.

Crafting a Compelling Vision and Effective Communication:

A compelling vision is both inspirational and attainable. It should resonate with the core values and goals of the organization, painting a vivid picture of what success looks like. Effective communication of this vision involves conveying it in a simple, memorable, and impactful manner. The vision should be repeated consistently and integrated into the organization's culture.

An exercise to craft a compelling vision involves envisioning your organization five to ten years from now. Describe what success looks like. Then, condense this description into a clear and concise vision statement. Once crafted, share this statement with a select group and gather their feedback for refinement.

Exercise for Visionary Leadership:

1. **Vision Board Creation:** Craft a vision board depicting your personal and professional aspirations. Include images, quotes, and symbols that represent your envisioned future. Display this board in your workspace to remind yourself daily of your goals.

2. **Future Letter to Yourself:** Write a letter to your future self, describing where you envision yourself in five years. Detail your achievements, experiences, and the impact you've made. Seal this letter and open it five years later to reflect on your journey.

3. **Storytelling for Vision Sharing:** Practice storytelling by narrating a compelling story that embodies your vision. Use this story to communicate your vision to your team or stakeholders. Effective storytelling enhances understanding and buy-in.

In conclusion, visionary leadership is the compass steering teams towards a shared destination. Let us craft our visions with care and articulate them with passion and precision. By illuminating the path ahead, we inspire greatness, achieving milestones that seemed distant, and guiding our teams towards a brighter future.

3. Building High-Performing Teams: Elevating Team Excellence

Building high-performing teams is like orchestrating a symphony where every instrument plays a vital role in creating a harmonious melody. Understanding the strategies to foster teamwork, collaboration, and a positive team culture is essential for every leader. Empowering team members to reach their full potential amplifies this melody, creating a symphony of excellence.

Strategies for Fostering Teamwork and Collaboration: Imagine a rowing team, synchronized in their strokes, propelling the boat forward swiftly. Teamwork and collaboration are the oars that power this boat of success. Establishing clear goals, roles, and responsibilities for each team member is crucial. Encouraging open communication, active listening, and valuing diverse perspectives create an environment where ideas flow freely.

For instance, Pixar Animation Studios is a testament to collaboration. Their "Braintrust" sessions involve a group of directors and creative minds critiquing and enhancing each other's work. This collaborative approach has been instrumental in their consistent creation of beloved animated films.

Techniques for Empowering Team Members:

Empowering team members involves providing them with autonomy, trust, and opportunities for growth. Recognizing and utilizing each individual's strengths, skills, and expertise fosters a sense of ownership and responsibility. A leader should also offer constructive feedback and provide resources for development.

A practical exercise to empower team members is the "Strengths-based Approach." Encourage team members to identify their strengths using assessments like Gallup's StrengthsFinder. Once identified, discuss how these strengths can be leveraged within the team to achieve collective goals.

Exercise to Foster a Positive Team Culture:

1. **Team Appreciation Circle**: Form a circle with team members. Starting with one member, each person appreciates the colleague on their right, highlighting their strengths and contributions. This fosters a positive environment and strengthens team bonds.

2. **Collaborative Project Simulation**: Divide the team into smaller groups and assign a hypothetical project. Each group collaboratively brainstorms, plans, and presents their approach. This exercise encourages teamwork, creativity, and problem-solving.

3. **Monthly Team Awards**: Institute monthly awards recognizing team members for various categories like 'Innovation Champion', 'Collaborator of the Month', or 'MVP (Minimum Viable Product)'. Celebrate the winners and their contributions, motivating others to excel.

In conclusion, building high-performing teams is an art that requires a blend of collaboration, empowerment, and a nurturing culture. Let us embrace these strategies and exercises, conducting our symphony of teamwork and empowerment, where every member's unique tune resonates, creating a masterpiece of collective success and fulfillment.

4. Ethical Leadership and Decision-Making: Guiding Light

Ethical leadership is the beacon that illuminates the path of integrity, fostering trust and credibility in every step. Understanding the role of ethical leadership in building these pillars is foundational for any leader. Equally important is mastering the approaches to ethical decision-making, especially in the face of complex ethical dilemmas, to ensure that each decision stands the test of moral scrutiny.

The Role of Ethical Leadership: Imagine a ship navigating through turbulent waters. Ethical leadership is the lighthouse guiding the ship safely to its destination. Leaders who embody and exemplify ethics in their actions, decisions, and interactions build trust and credibility. Their conduct becomes a compass for the entire organization, steering it towards a culture of honesty, fairness, and responsibility.

For instance, Microsoft's CEO, Satya Nadella, emphasizes the importance of ethical leadership in the age of technology. He advocates for a culture that prioritizes privacy, security, and transparency, ensuring the responsible use of technology and data.

Approaches to Ethical Decision-Making:

Ethical decision-making is a process that involves considering the moral implications of actions and choosing what is right and just. The ethical decision-making framework often involves evaluating actions based on ethical principles such as justice, fairness, honesty, and the well-being of stakeholders.

A practical exercise to enhance ethical decision-making involves the "Four-Way Test" method. Before making a decision, ask these four questions:

1) Is it the truth?

2) Is it fair to all concerned?

3) Will it build goodwill and better relationships?

4) Will it be beneficial to all concerned?

Evaluating decisions against these criteria helps in discerning the ethical implications.

Exercise for Navigating Ethical Dilemmas:

1. Case Study Analysis: Present team members with hypothetical or real ethical dilemmas related to your industry. Encourage them to analyze the cases, identify the ethical issues, and propose the most ethical course of action. This exercise hones their critical thinking in ethics.

2. Ethics Committee Simulation: Divide the team into groups and assign each group a different ethical dilemma. Have them simulate an ethics committee meeting, discussing, and debating the dilemma to reach a consensus on the most ethical solution.

3. Personal Values Reflection: Ask team members to reflect on their personal values and ethical principles. Provide scenarios and ask how their values guide their decision-making in those situations. This exercise helps in aligning personal values with ethical decision-making. In conclusion, ethical leadership is the moral compass that guides us through the labyrinth of choices. Let us embrace these strategies and exercises, ensuring that our decisions are steeped in integrity and righteousness. By doing so, we illuminate the path for ourselves and others, building a legacy of trust, credibility, and ethical excellence.

5

Harnessing Technology for Success

Mastering Tech: Leveraging Tools and Strategies for Optimal Success

"Technology is just a tool. In terms of getting the kids working together and motivating them, the teacher is the most important."

- Bill Gates

In this chapter, we explore how young professionals can leverage technology to drive success and innovation in their roles. Participants will gain insights into emerging trends and tools that can enhance their performance and efficiency.

Topics covered include:

1. Embracing Digital Transformation:

a) Understanding the significance of digital transformation in modern organizations.

b) Strategies for adapting to technological changes and staying relevant.

2. Maximizing Productivity with Tools:

a) Exploring productivity-enhancing tools and software for professionals.

b) Tips for integrating these tools into daily workflows.

3. Cybersecurity and Data Protection:

a) The importance of Cybersecurity awareness and data protection best practices.

b) Techniques for safeguarding sensitive information and mitigating risks.

4. Leveraging Artificial Intelligence:

a) How AI technologies can optimize processes and decision-making in business.

b) Ethical considerations in AI adoption and usage.

1. Embracing Digital Transformation: Pioneering Success through Technology

In the era of rapid digital evolution, embracing technological advancements is the key to unlocking success and staying ahead in the race. Understanding the significance of digital transformation and developing strategies to adapt to these changes is akin to skillfully navigating a ship through rapidly changing currents towards the vast ocean of opportunities.

Understanding the Significance of Digital Transformation: Imagine a sailboat harnessing the wind's power; digital transformation is that wind propelling an organization towards its goals. It's not just about adopting the latest technologies but reshaping the entire organizational mindset and processes. From enhanced productivity to improved customer experiences, digital transformation is the linchpin that defines the modern competitive landscape.

For instance, Amazon, with its digital transformation initiatives like AI-driven recommendations and efficient supply chain management, has redefined the online retail space. This transformation enabled them to cater to customer needs effectively and attain remarkable growth.

Strategies for Adapting to Technological Changes:

Adapting to technological changes requires a proactive approach. Firstly, fostering a culture of continuous learning and upskilling is imperative. Team members need to be equipped with the necessary skills to embrace new technologies. Additionally, promoting collaboration and cross-functional teamwork enhances innovative thinking and problem-solving.

A practical exercise involves a "Tech Innovation Challenge" for your own growth. Research and propose innovative ways to integrate a specific emerging technology (e.g., AI, blockchain, IoT (Internet of Things), UPI, Cloud, ChatGPT, GenAI) into the existing business model. This exercise fosters creativity and a deeper understanding of technological possibilities.

Exercise for Technological Adaptability:

1. **30-Day Tech Challenge**: Dedicate 30 days to explore a new technology or tool each day. Start with basic digital tools like productivity apps, then gradually move on to more advanced ones. Experiment, learn, and note how each tool can enhance your efficiency or skills.

2. **Tech Detox and Reflection**: Choose a weekend for a 'tech detox.' Disconnect from all digital devices and platforms. Engage in offline activities like reading, outdoor walks, or journaling. Reflect on how this break affected your well-being and interactions.

3. **Digital Journal of Insights**: Maintain a digital journal to document your insights about the technological changes around you. Include news articles, personal reflections, and ideas on how these changes could impact your personal and professional life. Regularly review and update this journal.

In conclusion, embracing digital transformation is not an option but a necessity in today's dynamic world. Let us seize the opportunities technology offers and navigate our organizations towards success. Through continuous learning and proactive adaptation, we ride the digital wave, steering our ship towards a future of innovation, growth, and sustainable success.

2. **Maximizing Productivity with Tools**: Elevating Efficiency & Empowering Professionals with Productivity Tools

In the contemporary professional landscape, individuals are akin to skilled artisans equipped with a toolbox of specialized instruments, each designed to boost productivity and streamline operations. Understanding and harnessing these productivity-enhancing tools is similar to acquiring a toolkit for success. Let's explore the world of such tools, comprehending their potential, and gaining insights into seamlessly integrating them into daily workflows.

Exploring Productivity-Enhancing Tools:

Imagine a seasoned chef's kitchen, well-stocked with an array of utensils and gadgets. Similarly, professionals have access to a variety of productivity tools that transcend industry boundaries. These tools cater to diverse needs, from communication platforms like Slack and Microsoft Teams to collaborative document editing in Google Workspace and creativity boosters like Canva. In recent years, AI tools like ChatGPT have also come to the forefront, transforming how professionals' access and process information.

For example, ChatGPT has revolutionized the way professionals interact with information. It can generate content, answer questions, and provide recommendations, making it a versatile tool for tasks ranging from content creation to research assistance.

Tips for Integrating These Tools into Daily Workflows:

Efficiently integrating productivity tools into daily workflows necessitates a strategic approach. Begin by comprehending the features and capabilities of the chosen tools. Personalize them to align with your specific workflow requirements. Encourage colleagues and team members to adopt these tools collaboratively. Provide training to ensure everyone can harness the full potential of these tools.

A practical exercise involves using AI tools like ChatGPT for research and content creation. For instance, task ChatGPT with summarizing a complex report or drafting a compelling blog post. Assess the tool's impact on your efficiency and output.

Exercise for Hands-on Learning:

a) **AI-Driven Research Challenge**: Select an AI research tool or platform like ChatGPT and utilize it to research a complex topic. Evaluate the quality and speed of information retrieval and how it contributes to your research process.

b) **Content Creation with AI**: Experiment with AI-powered content creation. Use an AI writing tool to draft a newsletter, social media posts, or marketing copy. Compare the time and quality of output with your usual content creation process.

c) **Data Analysis Simulation**: Use a data analytics tool with AI capabilities to analyze a dataset related to your business. Extract insights, trends, and patterns. Evaluate how this tool streamlines the data analysis process.

In conclusion, productivity tools are the foundation on which professionals build their path to excellence. Let us embrace these strategies and exercises, ensuring we wield these tools skillfully. Through this, we unlock a world of efficiency, propelling ourselves towards achievements beyond our imagination, regardless of our industry or field of expertise.

3. Cybersecurity and Data Protection: Safeguarding Your Digital World

In this digital age, protecting your personal information is like securing your home. Just as we lock our doors to keep intruders out, we must safeguard our digital space to keep our information safe. Let's dive into the world of cybersecurity and data protection, understanding why it's essential and how to shield our valuable data.

The Importance of Cybersecurity Awareness and Data Protection:

Imagine you have a treasure chest. This chest holds your important documents, memories, and valuables. Now, think of the internet as a vast sea. Cybersecurity is like a strong lock on this chest, ensuring that only you have the key. It's vital to be aware of potential threats and understand how to use that lock effectively.

For example, securing your email with a strong, unique password is a basic step. It's like locking the door to your home. Additionally, being cautious about the emails you open and not sharing sensitive information with unknown sources is akin to not letting strangers into your house.

Techniques for Safeguarding Sensitive Information and Mitigating Risks:

Think of your personal information as precious gems. You wouldn't leave them lying around, right? Likewise, be mindful of what you share online. Use strong, unique passwords for your accounts - it's like having a special combination lock for each gem. Regularly update your devices and apps to add an extra layer of protection, just as you would reinforce the walls of your home.

A practical exercise involves reviewing your social media privacy settings. Imagine social media is like a window to your home. Adjust the blinds (privacy settings) to control what others can see. Understand what information you're sharing and who can access it.

Exercise for Personal Data Protection:

1. Password Workout: Assess and strengthen your passwords. Think of a strong, memorable phrase, and use the initials, numbers, and symbols to create your password. For example, "I love hiking in 2023!" can become "IL0veH1k!ng!n2023!."

2. App Permissions Check-up: Review app permissions on your phone. Go through the list of apps and disable unnecessary permissions. If a

photo-editing app doesn't need access to your contacts, revoke that permission.

3. **Phishing Spotting:** Learn to spot phishing emails. Practice identifying red flags like generic greetings, misspellings, and suspicious links. Imagine it's like learning to recognize a suspicious person at your doorstep.

In conclusion, cybersecurity is like building a fence around your information, ensuring it's safe from prying eyes. Let's embrace these strategies and exercises, ensuring we shield our digital treasures effectively. By doing so, we create a digital fortress, protecting what matters most in our virtual world.

4. Leveraging Artificial Intelligence: Efficiency and Ethics

Artificial Intelligence (AI) is like a trusted advisor, ready to enhance processes and decision-making across various domains. Understanding the transformative potential of AI and the ethical considerations surrounding its adoption is crucial. Let's explore how AI can be a game -changer and how to tread this path responsibly.

How AI Technologies Can Optimize Processes and Decision-Making:

Imagine having a tireless assistant who can analyze vast amounts of data and provide insights instantaneously. AI serves as this virtual assistant across industries. In healthcare, AI aids in diagnosing diseases by analyzing medical images. In finance, it predicts market trends, optimizing investments. In marketing, it personalizes recommendations, boosting customer engagement.

For example, consider Netflix's recommendation system. It uses AI to analyze your viewing habits and preferences, suggesting content tailored to your taste. This AI-driven personalization keeps viewers engaged and satisfied.

Ethical Considerations in AI Adoption and Usage:

AI is powerful, but with great power comes great responsibility. Ethical considerations in AI usage are akin to the principles guiding a just society. Privacy, fairness, transparency, and accountability must be at the forefront of AI adoption. For instance, facial recognition technology has raised ethical concerns related to privacy and surveillance. Companies and policymakers are now working to establish guidelines and regulations for its responsible use.

Exercise for Ethical AI Reflection:

a) **AI Impact Assessment:** Choose an AI application relevant to your domain (e.g., chatbots for customer service). Reflect on its potential impact, both positive and negative. Consider how it may affect individuals, society, and your organization. Identify potential ethical challenges.

b) **AI Ethics Discussion:** Organize a group discussion or seminar within your team or organization. Select an AI-related topic (e.g., bias in AI algorithms) and encourage participants to share their thoughts and concerns. Facilitate a dialogue to raise awareness of ethical issues.

c) **Ethical Scenario Discussion:** Engage in group discussions or workshops where you discuss hypothetical scenarios involving AI. Explore ethical dilemmas and brainstorm solutions to ensure fair and responsible AI usage

In conclusion, AI is a powerful tool, like a double-edged sword. Let us harness its potential to optimize processes and decision-making while remaining vigilant about ethical considerations. By embracing these strategies and exercises, we ensure that AI becomes a force for good, contributing to a more efficient and ethically sound future.

6

Nurturing Resilience and Coping with Change

Thriving Through Turbulence:

Building Resilience and Embracing Change

"You may encounter many defeats, but you must not be defeated. In fact, it may be necessary to encounter the defeats so you can know who you are, what you can rise from, how you can still come out of it."

- Maya Angelou

In this chapter, readers will discover the importance of resilience in navigating challenges and uncertainties in their careers. We explore strategies to cope with change and adapt to evolving work environments.

Topics covered include:

1. Building Resilience:

a) Understanding resilience as a critical skill in overcoming setbacks and adversity.

b) Techniques to develop resilience and bounce back stronger after challenges.

2. Coping with Change:

a) Strategies to embrace change positively and thrive in dynamic workplaces.

b) Mindset shifts to view change as an opportunity for growth.

3. Stress Management for Professionals:

a) Recognizing stress triggers and its impact on performance and well-being.

b) Practical stress reduction techniques for a healthier work-life balance.

4. Cultivating Mental Well-Being:

a) The role of mindfulness and self-care in maintaining mental wellness.

b) Techniques for fostering a positive and supportive work environment.

1. Building Resilience: Rising Strong

In the tempestuous seas of life, resilience stands tall as the lighthouse that guides us through the storm. Understanding resilience as a critical skill is paramount in our voyage to overcome setbacks and adversity. It's the pillar that enables us to weather the strongest of gales and emerge stronger and wiser.

Understanding Resilience: The Bedrock of Endurance

Resilience is not merely about bouncing back from tough situations; it's about navigating them skillfully and bouncing forward. It's the art of bending without breaking, adapting to change, and maintaining one's equilibrium amidst life's challenges. Resilience stems from a combination of mental fortitude, emotional intelligence, and a positive outlook.

Imagine a successful entrepreneur whose business faced a major crisis due to a sudden economic downturn. Instead of succumbing to the pressure, this entrepreneur utilized resilience. They assessed the situation, recalibrated their strategy, and emerged from the crisis with an even stronger and more diversified business portfolio.

Techniques to Develop Resilience: Forging Inner Strength

a) Mindfulness and Emotional Regulation: Practice mindfulness to stay present and composed during challenging times. Understand and regulate your emotions. Embrace your feelings, analyze them, and channel them into productive actions.

b) Positive Self-Talk and Optimism: Cultivate a positive internal dialogue. Replace negative thoughts with constructive ones. Optimism acts as a shield against pessimism, helping you navigate through adversity with a hopeful perspective.

c) **Flexible Thinking and Adaptability:** Train your mind to be flexible and adaptive. Be open to change and embrace uncertainty. Recognize that change is a constant and adaptability is the key to resilience.

d) **Social Support and Connection:** Build a strong support network of friends, mentors, or support groups. Sharing your experiences and challenges with others can provide fresh perspectives and emotional relief.

The Resilience Journal: Create a 'Resilience Journal' to document your journey towards building resilience.

a) **Daily Resilience Reflection:** At the end of each day, jot down the challenges you faced, your emotional reactions, and how you managed them. Reflect on what you learned and how you can respond more resiliently in the future.

b) **Identifying Resilience Role Models:** Identify individuals you consider resilient. Analyze their behaviors and approaches to challenges. Note down the traits you'd like to adopt and integrate into your own life.

c) **Setting Resilience Goals:** Set short-term and long-term goals to enhance your resilience. Define actionable steps to achieve these goals. Regularly track your progress and adjust your approach if needed.

In conclusion, resilience is the beacon that guides us through life's stormy seas. By understanding its essence and embracing the techniques to cultivate it, we can transform adversity into opportunities for growth. Let us set sail on the journey of resilience, emerging from challenges not just strong but stronger. For in the face of adversity, we rise, we learn, and we conquer.

2. Coping with Change: A Journey of Growth and Resilience

In the tapestry of life, change is the thread that weaves the story of our growth and evolution. Coping with change isn't just a skill; it's an art that empowers us to thrive in dynamic workplaces and navigate the ebb and flow of life. It's about not merely adapting to change but embracing it with open arms, seeing it as an opportunity for personal and professional growth.

Strategies to Embrace Change Positively: Shifting Sails Towards Growth

a) **Cultivate a Growth Mindset:** View challenges and changes as opportunities to learn and develop. A growth mindset allows you to adapt and thrive in changing circumstances, enabling you to see possibilities instead of roadblocks.

b) **Continuous Learning and Upskilling:** Stay updated with the latest trends and advancements in your field. Embrace learning as a lifelong journey. Attend workshops, enroll in courses, and seek opportunities to broaden your skill set.

c) **Effective Communication:** In times of change, clear communication is key. Keep the lines of communication open with colleagues and superiors. Express your thoughts, concerns, and ideas constructively. Understanding the 'why' behind change often eases the transition.

d) **Resilience and Adaptability:** Develop resilience to bounce back from setbacks swiftly. Adaptability is your sail in the storm, allowing you to adjust to new situations and find effective solutions.

Example: The Transformational Journey of a Tech Company

Consider a tech company that decided to shift its focus from traditional software to Artificial Intelligence and Machine Learning.

This change impacted every aspect of the organization - from the skill sets required to the company's culture. While it was a significant change, employees embraced it as an opportunity for growth. They engaged in upskilling programs, fostering a culture of continuous learning and adaptability. Consequently, the company not only survived but thrived in the competitive tech landscape, emerging as a leader in AI-driven solutions.

Change Navigator: Sailing Towards Growth

a) **Change Reflection Journal:** Start a 'Change Reflection Journal'. Whenever you encounter a change, jot down your initial thoughts and emotions regarding the change. Then, list potential opportunities and positive outcomes that may arise from this change. Regularly revisit your entries to track your evolving perspective.

b) **Change Impact Assessment:** Assess the impact of a significant change in your life or workplace. Identify the aspects that will be affected - skills, relationships, routines. Propose strategies to mitigate negative impacts and capitalize on positive aspects of the change.

c) **Monthly Change Challenge:** Every month, challenge yourself to embrace a small change in your routine. It could be something as simple as trying a new workout routine or altering your commute. Reflect on how you adapted and what you learned from this change.

In conclusion, change is not a force to be feared but a current that propels us towards growth and excellence. By adopting strategies to embrace change positively and shifting our mindset, we can navigate the waves of change with grace. Let us set sail with resilience and adaptability, for in the sea of change lies the treasure of our true potential.

3. Stress Management for Professionals: Mastering Balance

In the modern professional landscape, where the pace is relentless and expectations are sky-high, understanding and managing stress is the compass that guides us towards calmer waters. Stress management isn't merely about alleviating the symptoms; it's about navigating the storm, recognizing stress triggers, and steering towards a healthier work-life balance.

Recognizing Stress Triggers: The Barometer of Resilience

Stress triggers vary from person to person, but they often stem from common sources like excessive workload, tight deadlines, conflicts at work, or even personal issues. It's essential to pinpoint these triggers to effectively manage stress. Listen to your body and mind. Is it the tightness in your chest when deadlines loom? The lack of focus when too many tasks pile up? Understanding these signs is the first step towards building resilience.

Impact on Performance and Well-being: The Ripple Effect

Stress doesn't just affect our emotional state; it ripples through our entire being, impacting our physical health, relationships, and professional performance. It clouds our decision-making abilities, saps our energy, and weakens our immune system. Chronic stress can lead to burnout and a myriad of health issues like high blood pressure, insomnia, and anxiety disorders.

Practical Stress Reduction Techniques: A Harbor in the Storm

a) **Mindfulness and Meditation:** Practice mindfulness to stay present and anchored. Simple breathing exercises and guided meditation can calm a racing mind and bring focus. Take short breaks during the day to practice deep breathing and reset.

b) **Physical Exercise**: Engage in regular physical activity like yoga, jogging, or even a brisk walk during lunch breaks. Exercise is a powerful stress reliever, releasing endorphins that boost mood and reduce stress.

c) **Time Management and Prioritization**: Organize your tasks using effective time management techniques. Prioritize tasks based on urgency and importance. Break down complex projects into manageable tasks and tackle them one step at a time.

d) **Healthy Lifestyle Choices**: Maintain a balanced diet, stay hydrated, and ensure adequate sleep. Avoid excessive consumption of caffeine and sugar, as they can contribute to heightened stress levels.

The Journey of a Financial Analyst

Imagine a financial analyst juggling multiple high-profile projects with strict deadlines. The pressure was immense, leading to chronic stress. Recognizing the toll it was taking on his performance and health, he adopted stress management techniques. Regular exercise and mindfulness practice became his anchors. He started prioritizing tasks and setting realistic goals. Gradually, his performance improved, and he found a healthier work-life balance.

Stress Diary and Action Plan:

a) **Stress Diary**: Maintain a stress diary for a week. Note down situations causing stress, your reactions, and physical sensations. Reflect on these entries to identify patterns and triggers.

b) **Stress Action Plan**: Based on your stress diary, create a stress action plan. List down stress reduction techniques you'll incorporate into your routine. Set achievable goals and a timeline for their implementation.

In conclusion, stress management isn't about avoiding stress; it's about equipping ourselves with strategies to navigate it effectively. Let us recognize our stress triggers, prioritize our well-being, and sail through the storms with resilience. Through these techniques, we can achieve a state of equilibrium, where we not only survive but thrive in the dynamic seas of the professional world.

4. Cultivating Mental Well-Being: Nurturing Serenity

In the bustling world of professionals, where targets and deadlines often take the spotlight, tending to our mental well-being is akin to nurturing a garden. Cultivating mental well-being isn't just a luxury; it's a necessity. Understanding the significance of mindfulness, self-care, and a positive work environment can be transformative in ensuring our minds remain serene amidst the chaos.

The Role of Mindfulness and Self-Care: Foundations of Well-being

Mindfulness is the art of being present, fully engaging with each moment. It's about acknowledging our thoughts and emotions without judgment. Self-care, on the other hand, involves nurturing our physical, emotional, and mental health. Both these practices form the bedrock of mental well-being.

Imagine a software engineer constantly facing tight project deadlines and dealing with complex code issues. Overwhelmed and stressed, she began practicing mindfulness during short breaks, focusing on her breath and letting go of anxious thoughts. Additionally, she started incorporating self-care routines like regular exercise and creative hobbies. These practices not only enhanced her mental well-being but also positively impacted her productivity at work.

Techniques for Fostering a Positive Work Environment: Seeds of Mental Wellness

a) **Encourage Open Communication**: Create an environment where employees feel safe to voice their concerns and ideas. Effective communication fosters a sense of belonging and reduces stress levels.

b) **Promote Work-Life Balance**: Encourage employees to maintain a healthy work-life balance by respecting their time outside of work hours. Avoid sending work-related emails or messages during non-working hours.

c) **Offer Professional Development Opportunities**: Provide opportunities for skill development and growth within the organization. Feeling stagnant in one's career can lead to stress and dissatisfaction.

d) **Recognize and Appreciate Efforts**: Acknowledge and appreciate the efforts and achievements of employees. Feeling valued boosts morale and overall mental well-being.

Gratitude Journal and Mindful Breaks

a) **Gratitude Journal**: Set aside a few minutes each day to write down three things you are grateful for. Reflect on the positive aspects of your life, no matter how small. Over time, this practice can shift your focus towards positivity.

b) **Mindful Breaks**: During your workday, dedicate a few minutes to a mindful break. Close your eyes, focus on your breath, and let go of any stressful thoughts. Return to your tasks with a rejuvenated mind.

In conclusion, nurturing our mental well-being is a responsibility we owe to ourselves and our work. Let us embrace mindfulness and self-care, understanding that a serene mind is a catalyst for productivity and happiness. By fostering a positive work environment, we sow the seeds of mental wellness, reaping the bountiful harvest of a flourishing professional life.

7

Networking and Building Professional Relationships

Building Bridges: Cultivating Meaningful Connections in Your Professional Journey

"Your network is your net worth. Building genuine relationships and supporting others can lead to unforeseen opportunities and exponential growth."

- Keith Ferrazzi

In this chapter, we explore the significance of networking for young professionals and how to build meaningful professional relationships that can enhance career prospects and opportunities.

Topics covered include:

1. The Power of Networking:

a) Understanding the value of networking for career growth and opportunities.

b) Tips for overcoming networking challenges and building genuine connections.

2. Leveraging social media for Professional Branding:

a) Utilizing social media platforms to showcase professional skills and achievements.

b) Crafting a compelling online presence to attract potential employers and collaborators.

3. Effective Networking Strategies:

a) Techniques for networking at conferences, events, and virtual environments.

b) How to leverage alumni networks, industry associations, and online communities.

4. Nurturing Mentoring Relationships:

a) The benefits of mentorship in career development and guidance.

b) Tips for seeking and fostering mentoring relationships with experienced professionals.

1. The Power of Networking: The Art of Connections

Networking is like planting seeds in a vast garden - each connection you nurture has the potential to grow into a beautiful opportunity. Let us delve into the world of networking, understanding its immense value in career growth, and learn how to overcome challenges to build meaningful and genuine connections.

Understanding the Value of Networking: Imagine you are a traveler, and each person you meet on your journey is a potential guide, showing you new paths and opportunities. Networking is just that - an avenue to meet individuals from diverse backgrounds, industries, and experiences. These connections can provide valuable insights, collaborations, job prospects, and a deeper understanding of your professional landscape.

For example, attending industry-specific networking events allows you to meet professionals who have navigated similar paths. Their experiences can offer invaluable advice, mentorship, or even partnership opportunities, which can significantly impact your career trajectory.

Tips for Overcoming Networking Challenges and Building Genuine Connections:

Networking can be intimidating, like stepping into a room full of strangers. However, it is important to remember that everyone is there for the same reason - to connect. Start with small steps, engage in conversations, and listen attentively. Authenticity is key; be genuinely interested in others and their stories.

A practical exercise involves joining an online networking platform or attending a virtual networking event related to your industry. Initiate a conversation with someone, sharing your professional interests and goals. Practice active listening and follow up with a thank-you note, solidifying the connection.

Exercise for Networking Skill Development:

a) **The Elevator Pitch:** Craft a concise and engaging introduction about yourself, highlighting your profession, passion, and what you seek. Practice delivering it within a minute - imagine you are in an elevator with a potential connection.

b) **Coffee Chat Challenge:** Reach out to a professional you admire and request a virtual coffee chat. Prepare thoughtful questions about their journey and industry. Treat it as a learning opportunity and a chance to forge a valuable connection.

c) **Networking Event Simulation:** Gather a group of fellow professionals and simulate a networking event. Role-play different scenarios, from approaching a contact to maintaining a conversation. This interactive exercise helps build confidence and networking skills.

In conclusion, networking is the bridge to new horizons in your professional journey. Let us embrace these strategies and exercises, ensuring we sow the seeds of genuine connections. Through this, we cultivate a garden of opportunities and learning, propelling ourselves towards a fulfilling and successful career.

2. Leveraging Social Media for Professional Branding:

In the modern professional landscape, social media is not just about connecting with friends; it is a powerful platform to showcase your skills and achievements, creating a spotlight for your professional brand. Let us delve into the world of leveraging social media for professional branding, understanding how to effectively showcase your expertise, and using AI tools like ChatGPT to augment your online presence.

Utilizing Social Media Platforms to Showcase Professional Skills and Achievements:

Imagine social media as a grand exhibition, and each post you share is like a masterpiece on display. Platforms like LinkedIn, Twitter, or

Facebook provide a stage to showcase your professional journey. Share success stories, projects you have worked on, or insights from your experiences. Engage with the community by participating in discussions, providing valuable insights, and highlighting your achievements.

For example, a marketing professional could share a campaign they spearheaded on LinkedIn, explaining the strategy, implementation, and outcomes. This not only showcases their skills but also establishes them as proficient marketers.

Crafting a Compelling Online Presence with AI Tools:

AI tools like ChatGPT can be your virtual collaborator in crafting compelling content. ChatGPT can help in writing engaging posts, creating insightful articles, or even refining your bio. It is like having a skilled co-writer, enhancing your content and making it more appealing to your audience.

A practical exercise involves creating a post with ChatGPT's assistance. Start with a topic related to your field, and let ChatGPT help you refine the content, ensuring it is informative and engaging. This exercise provides hands-on experience in using AI to enhance your online presence.

Exercise for Enhancing Your Digital Persona:

a) ChatGPT Content Refinement: Draft a post about a recent achievement or project. Use ChatGPT to refine the language and structure, making it more captivating and professional.

b) AI Content Calendar: Use AI tools to create a content calendar for the upcoming month. Collaborate with AI to generate ideas and even schedule posts, optimizing your social media presence.

c) **Community Engagement Challenge:** Engage with a relevant professional community on social media. Comment on posts, share your insights, and actively participate in discussions to bolster your online presence and expand your network.

In conclusion, social media is the stage where your professional brand can take the center spotlight. Let us embrace these strategies and exercises, integrating AI tools to refine and amplify our digital presence. Through this, we create a captivating narrative, attracting potential employers and collaborators to the enriching story of our professional journey.

3. Effective Networking Strategies: Mastering Connections

Networking is the compass that guides you through the professional landscape, helping you navigate with purpose and build meaningful connections. Let us explore effective networking strategies, understanding techniques for in-person and virtual environments, and discover the power of leveraging alumni networks, industry associations, and online communities.

Techniques for Networking at Conferences, Events, and Virtual Environments

Picture a conference or a virtual event as a bustling marketplace of opportunities. Engage by asking questions, actively listening, and sharing your insights. Be prepared with a succinct introduction, conveying who you are and what you do. Collect and exchange business cards or social media handles to stay connected post-event.

For instance, at a technology conference, initiate conversations about the latest trends. Share your experiences in the tech industry and inquire about others' perspectives. These exchanges can lay the foundation for future collaborations or job opportunities.

How to Leverage Alumni Networks, Industry Associations, and Online Communities

Alumni networks, industry associations, and online communities are treasure troves of potential connections. Alumni networks offer a shared background, making it easier to initiate conversations. Industry associations provide a platform to connect with like-minded professionals. Online communities, whether on social media or specialized platforms, offer a vast pool of professionals passionate about a common interest.

For example, consider a marketing professional wanting to expand their network. They can leverage their alumni network, join a marketing industry association, and participate in online marketing communities. Each avenue offers unique networking opportunities and a chance to collaborate with professionals in their field.

Exercise for Networking Skill Development:

a) **Event Buddy Challenge:** Attend a virtual event or conference and identify someone to be your "event buddy." Share your networking goals and check-in with each other throughout the event. Post-event, discuss your experiences and the connections you made.

b) **LinkedIn Engagement Experiment:** Engage with three different LinkedIn posts from your network or industry groups. Comment with thoughtful insights or questions to spark meaningful conversations and broaden your professional network.

In conclusion, effective networking is about fostering genuine connections and nurturing them for mutual growth. Let us embrace these strategies and exercises, enabling us to master the art of networking. Through this, we enrich our professional journey, paving the way for collaboration, opportunities, and a stronger, interconnected professional community.

4. Nurturing Mentoring Relationships: Guiding Lights for Career Growth

Mentorship is like having a guiding light in the journey of your career. It is a vital force that can propel you towards success and growth. Let us delve into the profound benefits of mentorship in career development and discover tips for seeking and fostering these invaluable relationships with experienced professionals.

The Benefits of Mentorship in Career Development and Guidance: Imagine your career as a challenging expedition. A mentor is like an experienced guide, showing you the way through treacherous terrain and providing invaluable wisdom. They share their experiences, offer constructive feedback, and help you navigate obstacles. A mentor's guidance can open doors to new opportunities, broaden your perspective, and accelerate your professional development.

For instance, a young entrepreneur starting a tech company might seek a mentor who has successfully built and scaled a tech startup. The mentor can provide insights on product development, marketing strategies, fundraising, and navigating the tech industry landscape.

Tips for Seeking and Fostering Mentoring Relationships with Experienced Professionals:

Seeking a mentor begins with identifying professionals whose journey and expertise align with your aspirations. Approach potential mentors respectfully and clearly communicate your goals and what you hope to gain from the relationship. Be proactive, show enthusiasm for learning, and respect their time and expertise.

Fostering a mentorship relationship involves being open to feedback, actively listening, and implementing the advice provided. Maintain regular communication and update your mentor on your progress.

Express gratitude for their guidance, as they are investing their time and knowledge in your growth.

Exercise for Building a Mentorship Approach:

a) **Mentor Research and Outreach:** Identify three professionals in your field whom you admire and would like as mentors. Research their work, achievements, and interests. Draft a respectful email or message introducing yourself and expressing your desire to learn from their expertise.

b) **Mentorship Goals Setting:** Reflect on your career goals and areas where you would like guidance. Write down specific objectives you aim to achieve through mentorship. Having clear goals will help guide discussions with your mentor.

c) **Networking Event Practice:** Attend a networking event or a professional meetup, aiming to engage with potential mentors or peers. Practice initiating conversations and expressing your interests and goals in a concise and engaging manner.

In conclusion, mentorship is a beacon that illuminates our professional path, enriching our journey. Let us embrace these strategies and exercises, enabling us to cultivate meaningful mentorship relationships. Through this, we navigate our careers with wisdom, continuously learning and growing under the guidance of these beacons of experience and knowledge.

8

Embracing Continuous Learning and Professional Growth

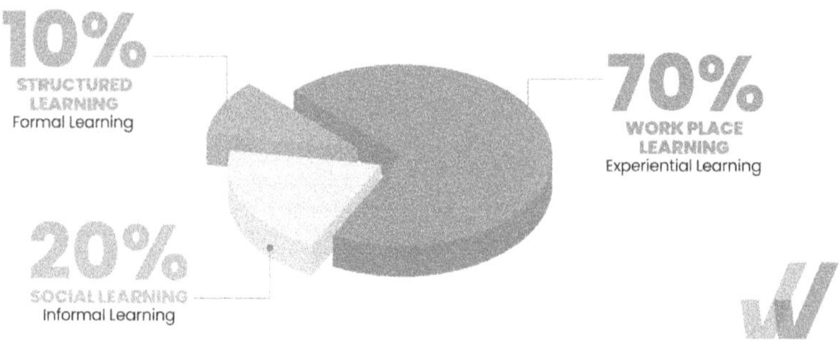

Unlocking Your Potential Through Lifelong Learning and Career Advancement

"Once you stop learning, you start dying. Embrace curiosity and let the pursuit of knowledge fuel your personal and professional growth."

- Albert Einstein

In our final chapter, we emphasize the importance of lifelong learning and continuous professional development. Participants will be encouraged to embrace a growth mindset and commit to their ongoing growth and success.

Topics covered include:

1. Embracing Lifelong Learning:

a) The significance of continuous learning in the ever-changing IT landscape.
b) Strategies for cultivating curiosity and staying updated with industry trends.

2. Identifying Learning Opportunities:

a) Discovering diverse learning resources, from online courses to workshops and conferences.
b) Tips for selecting learning opportunities that align with individual career goals.

3. Creating a Personal Development Plan:

a) Developing a structured plan for continuous professional growth.
b) Setting milestones and evaluating progress in achieving learning objectives.

4. Balancing Work, Learning, and Life:

a) Techniques for integrating learning into daily routines and work commitments.
b) Nurturing a growth-oriented mindset for long-term career success.

1. Embracing Lifelong Learning: Navigating the Ever-Evolving Business Landscape

In today's fast-paced business world, the journey of learning is an unending expedition. Let us delve into the profound significance of continuous learning in the ever-changing business landscape and explore effective strategies to cultivate curiosity, ensuring we stay updated with industry trends.

The Significance of Continuous Learning in the Ever-Changing Business Landscape:

Visualize the business landscape as a dynamic ecosystem, constantly evolving and adapting. Continuous learning acts as the compass, steering professionals and entrepreneurs through this ever-changing terrain. The business world is influenced by technological advancements, shifting consumer behaviors, and global trends. To thrive, one must commit to a lifelong learning mindset, keeping pace with innovations, market demands, and emerging opportunities. Lifelong learners adapt quickly, stay relevant, and seize new prospects.

For instance, consider the rise of e-commerce. Businesses that embraced digital transformation and continuously educated their teams on the latest trends and technologies found themselves gaining a competitive edge in the market.

Strategies for Cultivating Curiosity and Staying Updated with Industry Trends:

Cultivating curiosity is akin to having a powerful telescope that enables us to see beyond the horizon. To stay updated, allocate time for regular reading, whether it is industry-specific articles, books, or reputable online courses. Actively engage with thought leaders through webinars, podcasts, or attending industry conferences. Joining professional communities and networks keeps you connected and provides insights into the latest trends. Experimentation, networking, and seeking mentorship are vital components of a continuous learning strategy.

A practical exercise involves creating a learning plan for the upcoming month. List the industry trends, skills, or knowledge areas you aim to explore. Allocate specific time slots in your calendar for these learning pursuits and track your progress.

Exercise for a Lifelong Learning Commitment:

a) **Book Swap and Review**: Organize a book swap with peers or colleagues focusing on business-related books. Each participant can read a different book and then share a summary and key takeaway, encouraging a diversity of learning.

b) **Industry Trends Debate**: Form a discussion group with fellow professionals and engage in a debate about the latest industry trends. Assign roles to participants to argue for or against a particular trend, stimulating critical thinking and informed discussions.

c) **Knowledge-Sharing Webinars**: Host a knowledge-sharing webinar within your organization or professional network. Invite experts to present on trending topics or best practices, fostering a culture of continuous learning and collaboration.

In conclusion, embracing lifelong learning is the cornerstone of success in the dynamic business landscape. Let us embrace these strategies and exercises, igniting our curiosity and commitment to knowledge. Through this, we not only navigate the complex business terrain but also thrive, achieving our goals and contributing meaningfully to the ever-evolving world of business.

2. **Identifying Learning Opportunities**: Identifying Tailored Learning Opportunities

In the vast landscape of personal and professional development, identifying the right learning opportunities is like finding treasures that can enrich your journey. Let us explore the art of discovering diverse learning resources, from online courses to workshops and conferences, and delve into tips for selecting opportunities that resonate with individual career aspirations.

Discovering Diverse Learning Resources:

Imagine the world of learning as a vibrant garden, with each learning resource as a unique blossom. The modern era offers a multitude of options - online platforms like Coursera, Udemy, edX, industry-specific workshops, conferences, mentorship programs, and educational webinars. These resources provide a rich array of knowledge and experiences. Online courses offer flexibility, enabling you to learn at your own pace and on various topics, while workshops and conferences provide immersive experiences and networking opportunities.

For instance, someone aspiring to enhance their digital marketing skills can enroll in a specialized online course, attend marketing conferences, and participate in webinars hosted by marketing experts. Each avenue contributes to their knowledge and skill set in a distinct way.

Tips for Selecting Learning Opportunities:

Choosing the right learning opportunity is like tailoring a suit - it should fit you perfectly. Start by assessing your current skills, identifying gaps, and setting clear learning goals. Consider the credibility of the source, relevance to your career aspirations, depth of content, and reviews or testimonials. Evaluate the mode of learning - whether it aligns with your learning style and schedule. Also, seek opportunities that encourage hands-on application and interaction.

A practical exercise involves creating a learning vision board. Visualize where you want to be in your career in the next year or two. Then, research and pin learning opportunities (courses, workshops, etc.) that align with this vision. This will help in setting clear learning goals and identifying suitable resources.

Exercise for Personalized Learning Exploration:

a) **Skill Gap Analysis:** Conduct a self-assessment of your skills and knowledge. Identify areas where you lack proficiency and need further learning. Make a list of these areas for targeted learning.

b) **Learning Opportunity Comparison:** Research two or three learning opportunities on the same topic (e.g., a digital marketing course on two different platforms). Compare the content, mode of instruction, reviews, and the skills you will acquire to choose the most suitable option.

c) **Peer Recommendations:** Reach out to peers or industry professionals for recommendations on learning resources. Engage in a discussion to understand their experiences and how a particular resource benefited them in their careers.

In conclusion, identifying learning opportunities is a compass guiding us towards growth and success. Let us embrace these strategies and exercises, customizing our learning journey. Through this, we unlock a world of possibilities, enriching our knowledge, and achieving our career aspirations.

3. Creating a Personal Development Plan:

In the journey of professional growth, having a personalized roadmap is akin to having a compass that guides you through the maze of opportunities and challenges. Let us explore the art of creating a personal development plan, developing a structured approach for continuous professional growth, and setting milestones to ensure the realization of learning objectives.

Developing a Structured Plan for Continuous Professional Growth:

Imagine your career as a garden, and a personal development plan as the blueprint for nurturing it. Just as a garden needs careful planning, timely watering, and proper care, so does your professional journey. A personal development plan outlines your career goals, the skills you need to acquire, the experiences you should seek, and the knowledge you should gain. It acts as a roadmap, providing direction and focus.

For example, consider a sales professional aspiring to climb the career ladder. Their personal development plan might include goals like mastering negotiation skills, completing a sales management course, attending industry conferences, and shadowing senior sales executives.

Setting Milestones and Evaluating Progress:

Milestones are like signposts on the road - they mark your progress and distance covered. Break down your learning objectives into smaller, achievable milestones. Assign specific timelines and measurable metrics to each milestone. Regularly evaluate your progress, celebrate your achievements, and adjust your plan if needed. This iterative process keeps you on track and motivated.

A practical exercise involves creating a sample personal development plan. Choose an area you want to grow in, whether it is leadership, technical skills, or communication. Set short-term and long-term goals, define milestones, and allocate time limits for each. Regularly review and modify this plan as you progress.

Exercise for a Structured Personal Development Plan:

a) Goal-Setting Challenge: Set three short-term and three long-term professional goals. Make them specific, measurable, achievable, relevant, and time-bound (SMART). Write them down and review them regularly.

b) **Milestone Tracking**: Choose one of your short-term goals. Break it down into actionable steps or milestones. Assign deadlines to each milestone and track your progress weekly. Adjust your timeline if necessary.

c) **Personal SWOT Analysis**: Conduct a personal SWOT (Strengths, Weaknesses, Opportunities, Threats) analysis. Identify how your strengths can help achieve your goals and how to mitigate weaknesses. Leverage opportunities and devise strategies to overcome threats.

In conclusion, a personal development plan is your compass in the professional world, guiding you towards success. Let us embrace these strategies and exercises, creating our roadmap to success. Through this, we unlock our potential, achieve our objectives, and carve a meaningful and rewarding professional journey.

4. **Balancing Work, Learning, and Life**: Harmonizing the Symphony of Life

In the orchestral composition of life, striking a harmonious balance between work, learning, and personal life is the key to a melodious tune. Let us explore the art of integrating learning seamlessly into daily routines and work commitments, nurturing a growth-oriented mindset essential for long-term career success.

Techniques for Integrating Learning into Daily Routines and Work Commitments:

Imagine learning as the gentle hum in the background of your day, seamlessly blending with the melody of work and life. Incorporate learning into your routine by leveraging small pockets of time. Listen to audiobooks or educational podcasts during your commute, read articles during breaks, or dedicate a few minutes before bedtime to an online course. Make it a habit to jot down insights and reflections, integrating the learning into your thought process.

For example, a marketing professional can listen to a marketing strategy podcast during their daily commute. The knowledge gained can be applied during work, enhancing their performance and contributing to their learning goals.

Nurturing a Growth-Oriented Mindset for Long-Term Career Success:

Cultivate a mindset that views every experience as an opportunity for growth. Embrace challenges as stepping stones to success. Reflect on your accomplishments and failures, extracting valuable lessons from each. Seek feedback from peers and mentors, valuing diverse perspectives. Always be curious and hungry for knowledge, continuously seeking ways to improve and evolve both personally and professionally.

A practical exercise involves journaling your growth journey. Regularly write about your learning experiences, challenges faced, and how you overcame them. Reflect on how these experiences contribute to your growth and adjust your goals and actions accordingly.

Exercise for Life-Long Learning Integration:

a) **Knowledge Snippets Challenge:** Set a goal to read or listen to at least one educational snippet each day (e.g., a short article, a TED talk, or a podcast episode). Summarize what you have learned and discuss it with a friend or colleague.

b) **Lunch and Learn:** Organize or participate in a "lunch and learn" session at your workplace. Encourage team members to share insights on a topic of interest, promoting a culture of continuous learning within your organization.

c) **Weekly Reflection and Goal Setting:** Every week, take some time to reflect on your recent experiences, both personal and professional. Set achievable learning goals for the following week, aligning them with your long-term career aspirations.

In conclusion, balancing work, learning, and life is an artful symphony. Let us embrace these strategies and exercises, weaving learning into the fabric of our daily routines. Through this, we create a melodious life tune, embracing growth and success as our harmonious refrain.

CONCLUSION

"Success is not final, failure is not fatal: It is the courage to continue that counts."

- Winston Churchil

Congratulations! You have now concluded an enriching expedition through the realms of personal and professional growth in our Book, "Unlock Your True Potential: The Path to Professional Growth." You have ventured into a world brimming with insights, strategies, and empowering stories designed to ignite the spark of excellence within you.

Our journey commenced with the fundamental principle of personal development — a journey of self-discovery and self-mastery. Recognizing and nurturing your strengths while acknowledging your limitations forms the bedrock of your progress. It is about steering the wheel of your life towards continuous improvement and meaningful achievements.

Effective communication emerged as another vital cornerstone in our odyssey towards success. Communication is more than words; it is a dynamic force shaping perceptions and paving the way for meaningful relationships. Mastering the art of effective communication empowers you to connect, inspire, and lead with influence.

Leadership took center stage in this expedition. It is not confined to titles or authority; it is a mindset and skills that can be nurtured by all. Effective leadership involves inspiring and collaborating, navigating challenges with wisdom, and rallying individuals around a shared vision.

This journey highlighted the dynamic nature of personal and career growth — unique, personal, and marked by challenges and triumphs. It is a journey of self-discovery in a world filled with opportunities for the daring. Each chapter provided practical exercises and real-life examples, enabling you to apply knowledge, cultivate habits, and drive success one step at a time.

As Albert Einstein wisely stated, "The only source of knowledge is experience." Our journey has been just that—practical, rooted in real-world experiences, and grounded in tangible strategies.

So, as we close this chapter of our journey, remember that your path to excellence has just begun. Armed with the knowledge, insights, and exercises you have discovered in this Book, the world is your canvas. Let the experiences you gather and the knowledge you gain shape not just your career, but your life.

Thank you for being a part of this empowering adventure. Together, we have illuminated the path to personal and career excellence, paving the way for future generations of leaders, dreamers, and doers. Onwards and upwards!